"Poetic, practical, and accessible, Lissa Coffey's beautiful and passionate translation is a must for anyone looking to bring the Bhagavad Gita into daily life."

--Gary Jansen
Author of *Life Everlasting* and *The 15-Minute Prayer Solution*

"The Bhagavad Gita, since the time of Emerson, Thoreau, and Walt Whitman, has stirred the American imagination with its powerful call to action. Lissa Coffey's new abridged version delights the reader with lilting rhyme, conveying the core teaching of Yoga found in the Gita: Act without attachment to the fruits. Know what is most important. Find time to meditate. Orient yourself toward the highest. Bravo!"

--Christopher Key Chapple
Doshi Professor of Indic and Comparative Theology and Director,
Master of Arts in Yoga Studies Loyola Marymount University

"Lissa's love of the Bhagavad Gita is so completely heart-felt in this beautiful translation. What I love most about Song Divine is that it makes the Gita accessible for all to enjoy and love as much as Lissa does."

--Madisyn Taylor
Co-Founder, Editor in Chief, DailyOM

"In this beautiful book, Lissa Coffey brings out a much-hidden secret of Vedanta: Words don't carry meaning, words carry effects. A word is a Veda if it can produce an effect says Vivekananda. Most seekers get lost in the meaning of the words of Bhagavad Gita. Lissa has given us a very simple and easy way to bring out the desired effect of experiencing Brahman. This could well be a new and much easier way of studying the Bhagavad Gita. Read it. You will be surprised."

--Sri Vishwanath
Author of *The Secret of Bhagavad Gita*
and founder of Bhagavad Gita University

"Lissa Coffey has dived deep into the Gita with her fearless dedication to extract its essence, transformed that essence into English verse, and then shared it with us in this wonderful book."

--Swami Mahayogananda
Vedanta Society of Southern California

LISSA COFFEY

SONG DIVINE

A New Lyrical Rendition of the Bhagavad Gita

Foreword by Swami Sarvadevananda
Art by Rajesh Nagulakonda

Published by

Bamboo Entertainment, Inc.

4607 Lakeview Canyon Road Suite 181

Westlake Village, CA 91361

songdivine.com

ISBN: 9781-883212-31-5

Design and DTP by Rajesh Nagulakonda

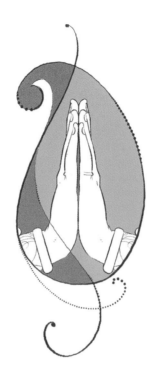

Dedicated to

Govinda

with loving devotion

CONTENTS

QUOTES ABOUT THE BHAGAVAD GITA

"When I read the Bhagavad-Gita and reflect about how God created this universe everything else seems so superfluous." -Albert Einstein

"I owed a magnificent day to the Bhagavad-gita. It was the first of books; it was as if an empire spoke to us, nothing small or unworthy, but large, serene, consistent, the voice of an old intelligence which in another age and climate had pondered and thus disposed of the same questions which exercise us." - Ralph Waldo Emerson

"When doubts haunt me, when disappointments stare me in the face, and I see not one ray of hope on the horizon, I turn to Bhagavad-gita and find a verse to comfort me; and I immediately begin to smile in the midst of overwhelming sorrow. Those who meditate on the Gita will derive fresh joy and new meanings from it every day." -Mahatma Gandhi

"In the morning I bathe my intellect in the stupendous and cosmogonal philosophy of the Bhagavad-gita, in comparison with which our modern world and its literature seem puny and trivial." -Henry David Thoreau

"The Bhagavad-Gita is a true scripture of the human race a living creation rather than a book, with a new message for every age and a new meaning for every civilization." -Sri Aurobindo

"The idea that man is like unto an inverted tree seems to have been current in by gone ages. The link with Vedic conceptions is provided by Plato in his Timaeus in which it states...' behold we are not an earthly but a heavenly plant.' This correlation can be discerned by what Krishna expresses in chapter 15 of Bhagavad-Gita." -Carl Jung

"The Bhagavad-Gita deals essentially with the spiritual foundation of human existence. It is a call of action to meet the obligations and duties of life; yet keeping in view the spiritual nature and grander purpose of the universe." -Jawaharlal Nehru, First Prime Minister of India

"The marvel of the Bhagavad-Gita is its truly beautiful revelation of life's wisdom which enables philosophy to blossom into religion." -Herman Hesse

"From a clear knowledge of the Bhagavad-Gita all the goals of human existence become fulfilled. Bhagavad-Gita is the manifest quintessence of all the teachings of the Vedic scriptures." -Adi Shankara

"The Bhagavad-Gita is the most systematic statement of spiritual evolution of endowing value to mankind. It is one of the most clear and comprehensive summaries of perennial philosophy ever revealed; hence its enduring value is subject not only to India but to all of humanity." -Aldous Huxley

"The Bhagavad-Gita has a profound influence on the spirit of mankind by its devotion to God which is manifested by actions." -Albert Schweitzer

FOREWORD

The Bhagavad Gita is a holy book for all times, places and cultures. It doesn't belong to one person, nor does it address any one group of people. It is a scripture for all the world and everyone in it, wherever they are in their spiritual quest.

The Bhagavad Gita has inspired many people with its powerful teachings and profound truths. It draws from the wisdom of the Upanishads, and wraps up all the essence of this wisdom as a practical guide to living. The deep spiritual lessons are as applicable in today's modern world as they were back in the time of Krishna, more than 5,000 years ago.

It's no wonder that the Bhagavad Gita, originally written in Sanskrit, is the second-most translated book in the world after the Bible. There are countless versions, in many different languages, and with a variety of commentaries on the verses. And now Lissa Coffey, or "Parama" as she is known to us here at the Vedanta Society, has brought us her own very special version of the Gita. This Gita is ideal for the western seeker in that the verses have rhythm, and they rhyme, making them very easy to both understand and memorize. Keeping the words of the Gita in the mind helps us to focus on what really matters in this life, and to remember the vital teachings that Krishna imparts to his friend Arjuna during their intense discussion on the battlefield.

The Bhagavad Gita is a part of the Mahabharata, a great epic filled with stories and philosophy. The Mahabharata contains 97,400 verses, while the Gita comes in at 700 verses. The Gita is said to be the spiritual core of the Mahabharata, expressing the same concepts in a much shorter narrative. Adi Sankaracharya, who consolidated the doctrine of Advaita Vedanta, was the first to recognize the greatness of the Bhagavad Gita, and wrote his wonderful commentary on it, thereby establishing the Gita as one of the fundamental texts of Vedanta.

The one theme that runs through the entire Bhagavad Gita is that the purpose of life is to realize our essential Being. In other words, to know and understand who we are, and why we are here on this earth. It may be called Enlightenment, Nirvana, Self-Realization, Awareness, Oneness – there are many different terms for this experience. But when we achieve it, we recognize that the experience, by any name, is the same for each of us.

I first met Lissa at the Vedanta Society in Santa Barbara. She quickly started attending our weekly Bhagavad Gita classes at the Hollywood Temple. Lissa, through her many books, has been able to bring some very big spiritual concepts to a mainstream audience by explaining them in a way that is easy to understand and also easy to apply to the modern-day lifestyle. I'm very pleased that Lissa has embraced the Gita in this way, and I know that many more people will be blessed with Krishna's valuable teachings because of her loving efforts in creating this book.

-Swami Sarvadevananda
Head Minister, The Vedanta Society of Southern California

INTRODUCTION

My own spiritual journey has been varied and unique, much like that of many of us in the western world these days. I was baptized in a Catholic church, spent holidays in a Lutheran church, and was always fascinated with all things mystical and spiritual, though I didn't know what to do with these thoughts. I remember memorizing the Lord's Prayer, not because anyone told me to but just because I wanted to. I also memorized the Hail Mary prayer. I think I was in the fifth grade at that time. During my UCLA years, I discovered meditation, and that experience opened up another world to me.

As an adult, I came across A Course in Miracles and fell in love with its beautiful philosophy. I studied it for many years and soaked in all the wisdom word by word. Later I became very active with what is now known as the Centers for Spiritual Living. This is a faith based organization that embraces all religions, so I dived right in, and enjoyed every minute of it. Then, as a student of Ayurveda, India's "Science of Life," I met Deepak Chopra, who introduced me to Vedanta. Vedanta spoke to me like nothing else ever had. I read everything I could get my hands on, and still wanted more. So, I ventured out to find a teacher, and spent time with several revered "gurus" who each had knowledge to share.

But in all of these places I felt there was something missing – I wasn't quite "at home" yet. Until I came to the Vedanta Society of Southern California, and I found my teacher in Swami Sarvadevananda. Now I'm at the Temple at least once a week, for hours on end! I love the community of students, the wonderful monks and nuns who teach the profound wisdom of Vedanta, and the beautiful space that is so warm and welcoming.

Over the years, I have collected many different variations of the Bhagavad Gita. For some reason, I was drawn to it, and I never knew why. When I was in India for my second trip, I was given another copy of the Bhagavad Gita as a gift. I took this as a sign, and started my studies. When Swami Sarvadevananda invited me to his Bhagatvad Gita class, I jumped at the opportunity. Learning these beautiful and profound spiritual truths has forever changed my life.

"Bhagavad Gita" translates from Sanskrit to mean "Song of God" or "Divine Song." It was written in verse, with rhythm and rhyme, so that it could be memorized and recited, or sung. However, that "beat" is lost when the words are translated into other languages, including English.

When my children were little, I quickly realized that the first words that kids memorize were words to a song. I couldn't find any songs made for kids that had the kind of inspirational, motivational words that I wanted them to remember and take to heart. So, I started writing songs myself, and started my own record label, recording albums, and later music videos for families. The words were meaningful, and the music catchy enough to not drive a parent crazy while listening to it in the car all day.

With this in mind, I thought that there must be some variation of the Bhagavad Gita that had been translated into English, that had both rhythm and rhyme, so that I could memorize the verses more easily. Swami Sarvadevananda always advised us about how wonderful it is to know the verses by heart, and encouraged us to memorize them. I set out to find such a translation, but came up empty. And that's when I decided to create it myself.

I kept this project a secret for a while, so that I could see if I could really do it. It was very important to me to be true to the original text, and yet have the book be accessible to someone who had not read it before. The task was quite overwhelming at first, but once I got into it, the words flowed, and I felt divinely guided. As research, I referred to many different versions of the Bhagavad Gita to make sure I understood the meaning behind the words properly. The version I relied on, and liked the most is the one by Swami Nikhilananda, founder of the Vedanta Society in New York.

The original Bhagavad Gita contains 700 verses. Mine contains 429, so it is a shortened version. What I've left out is a lot of the background history about the families involved in the war that comes in Chapter One and the first part of Chapter Two. There are also a few other characters in the Bhagavad Gita, but I chose to focus on Krishna and Arjuna exclusively as it is in their dialogue that we find all of the spiritual lessons. I've also left out some of the verses that explain the caste system, as I felt that this didn't apply to a modern, western audience.

I wanted powerful illustrations to go with the book. So, of course, I turned to the internet, and found some amazing drawings of Krishna. I tracked down the artist through Facebook, and approached Rajesh Nagulakonda. Rajesh told me of his love of mythology and art, and showed me some more of his work. I knew I had found the right man for the job! I gave him verses from each chapter and he used his unique artistic expression to convey the spiritual messages contained in each one. I love that all of these illustrations are such a unique blend of east and west, ancient and modern, and provide yet another aspect to the words.

The story takes place on a battlefield in Kurukshetra, located just north of Delhi in India, more than 5,000 years ago. The battle is between two sets of cousins, the Pandavas, to which the warrior Arjuna belongs and is to fight, and the Kauravas. Duryodhana is the head of the Kauravas army, and the evil son of the blind king Dhrtarastra. The Kauravas have taken over the Pandavas' kingdom. After all attempts at reconciliation have failed, the Pandavas are forced to fight back.

Krishna, worshipped as the eighth incarnation, or avatar, of the Hindu god Vishnu, was a revered god in his own right as well, though he also lived as a man, the king of Mathura, at the time of the war. As a close family friend to both sides, Krishna tried to intervene and prevent the war, to no avail. So, Krishna refused to bear arms in the battle or take a side. Instead, to make it a fair fight, he offered the loan of his army to one side, and his personal attendance to the other side. Krishna allowed Arjuna to make the first choice. Arjuna chose Krishna, his friend and mentor, to be by his side as his charioteer on the Pandavas side. The Kauravas thought Arjuna made a foolish choice, and were delighted to get the use of Krishna's powerful army.

The night before the battle is set to begin, Arjuna asks Krishna to drive him in the chariot between the two armies so he can get some perspective on the encounter with which he is confronted. Seeing the faces of his family, friends, teachers, and neighbors on the opposing side, Arjuna is overcome with confusion and despair. He sees that the Pandavas are outnumbered by the Kauravas, who also have more weaponry. He struggles with questions about the battle, and his own role in it. In this time of mental crisis, he desperately turns to Krishna for answers, for clarity. Krishna, seeing that Arjuna is sincere, open, and ready for this knowledge, patiently explains to his friend everything he needs to know. It is as if time stands still while these two have their conversation, and there is calm amongst the chaos.

Although the story takes place on a battlefield, it is really about the battles we are faced with in our own lives every day. Arjuna represents the common man, the working man, and every one of us. We are constantly presented with choices that we don't want to make. We are torn between what we think is good, and what is actually good for us. We are influenced by our desires and ambitions. The head fights with the heart, the intellect fights with the mind and senses.

When we come across these challenges, we tend to look outside ourselves for solutions. We want to place blame, to look for some kind of an "out." But this never works, and the problems only grow larger. What we need to do is, like Arjuna, get a new perspective by seeing each of the oppositions, the sources of conflict with which we are presented. And then dive deep into our own being, turn within. We each have a dharma, a purpose in this life. We each have a calling. When we understand our purpose, it gives us the strength to fight any battle. All of our life's solutions are found within.

Now, probably more than ever, what we are all searching for is peace of mind. We want to be happy, and to be successful. We strive feverishly to obtain whatever it is outside of us that we think it will take to make us happy or successful. But what we don't understand is that peace of mind is where it all starts. When the mind is calm and tranquil, despite any conditions or situations that we are in, then this provides fertile ground on which happiness and success can grow.

It is my wish that the Song Divine, the Bhagavad Gita, with Krishna's wise and beautiful words, helps you to know who you are. There's nothing more important than that. Know who you are, and the peace of mind that you have been seeking is yours.

Life's Lament

सीदन्ति मम गात्राणि मुखं च परिशुष्यति ।
वेपथुश्च शरीरे मे रोमहर्षश्च जायते ॥ १-२९ ॥

ARJUNA:

This is the calm before the storm,
Set into play before I was born.
This is the time to take a breath,
Before the hour will call for death.

My steady heart begins to race -
How did I get into this place?
This is not what I had planned.
Things got too far out of hand.

Do I even have a choice?
Do I even have a voice?
This opponent is not my enemy-
This opponent is my family.

I am a warrior, it's true.
But I don't know what to do.
I'm supposed to fight this fight,
But I'm not sure it is right.

They outnumber us, and they are strong.
But they are selfish, and they are wrong.
I'm conflicted, why must I kill?
Instead of rage I am feeling guilt.

With them in charge, it would be hell on earth
All we've worked for would have no worth.
But if I step up I'll live in hell – it's a sin
To murder my neighbors, to kill my kin.

This war is against my beliefs.
My conscience wants to feel relief.
Should I draw my weapon, and kill or die?
Or is the cost of battle just too high?

With so much against me, how can I win?
I might as well call it before war begins.
And yet the fight in my head won't leave me alone
I need a decision that I can own.

My body quivers, my hair stands on end.
The bow Gandiva slips from my hand.
I'd rather surrender, give up my own life,
Than by my actions create even more strife.

Tell me, dear Krishna, my advisor and friend –
How can I make this agony end?
I need your wisdom, what should I do?
Tell me, O Krishna, I'm begging you.

I need your wisdom, what shall I do?
Tell me, O Krishna, I'm begging you.

Know Who You Are

वासांसि जीर्णानि यथा विहाय
नवानि गृह्णाति नरो ऽपराणि ।
तथा शरीराणि विहाय जीर्णान्य्
अन्यानि संयाति नवानि देही ॥२-२२॥

KRISHNA:
Do you know who you are?
Do you know from where you came?
When you understand the Truth
Life will never be the same.

Never was there a time
When there was not a we –
Never will there come a time
When any of us cease to be.

You are not this body,
This garment that gets shed.
You are what continues
When the body turns up dead.

Just as the soul continues through,
When the body goes through stages,
Souls pass to a new body like
It does when the body ages.

A person casts off worn-out clothes
And those that he's outgrew.
The Soul casts off a worn-out shell
And enters into one that is new.

Death is certain for the body
And for this you should not grieve,
The Atman, who dwells in each of us
Is indestructible and free.

Notions of heat and cold arise,
Like those of pain and pleasure.
They come and go, they never stay -
Endure as the senses measure.

Be calm amidst these changes,
Know that the unreal doesn't last.
The Real never ceases to be -
Hold on to this wisdom fast.

The Atman can't be cut or burnt,
It can't be wet or withered.
Eternal, all-pervading,
It is the same forever.

This Self is the one that's you,
Unmanifest, unchanging.
Therefore, knowing It to be so
You won't waste your time grieving.

Death comes to all those who are born,
It is unavoidable.
Then birth comes to those who die
As a part of the karmic cycle.

But the Self, dwelling in all bodies,
Never dies, and cannot be slain.
Though the body may be wounded,
The Soul doesn't feel any pain.

Consider your own dharma,
From which you should not waver.
Do your duty, as a warrior -
Don't refuse this righteous labor.

Fight as you have said you would,
Your very honor is at stake.
Do your best, and fight for what's good,
There are no errors you can make.

If you're killed, you'll go to heaven,
If you win, you'll enjoy the earth.
Therefore, arise, Arjuna,
And resolve to show your worth!

You can control your actions,
So do your very best.
But you can't control the outcome
Trust Brahman to do the rest.

Go beyond the extremes of life,
Break from the chains that hold you back.
Devoted to union with Brahman,
You'll see there's nothing that you lack.

ARJUNA:
How can a man have so much faith?
How does he look, how does he speak?
Of course, I want this same freedom,
How could this ever come to me?

KRISHNA:
One who casts off all desires,
Unperturbed by adversity,
Free from all attachment and fear
Is filled with wisdom steady.

The illumined withdraw the senses
As a tortoise draws in its limbs,
Freed from the objects of senses,
All wisdom is fixed in him.

The person with self-control,
With the senses under restraint,
Attains serenity of mind,
Free from attachment and hate.

Without longing, free from desire,
Seeing what is constant and true,
Devoid of the sense of "I" and "mine"
This peace can come to you, too.

Selfless Action

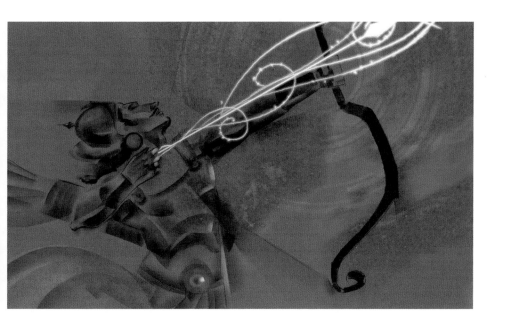

श्रेयान्स्वधर्मो विगुणः परधर्मात्स्वनुष्ठितात् ।
स्वधर्मे निधनं श्रेयः परधर्मो भयावहः ॥ ३-३५ ॥

ARJUNA:
My mind is reeling.
I hear what you say.
But is it knowledge that will save us,
Or is there some other way?

You speak to me of action –
Telling me that I must fight.
But if knowledge is the highest
Then this war doesn't seem right.

Is it one thing or the other?
How can I resolve these two?
Just give me some direction –
Just one thing that I can do.

KRISHA:
What you really want is freedom.
For everyone, that is the same.
To be free from all the ties that bind,
That keep us tethered to this game.

There are two ways to gain this freedom,
That you so desperately seek.
They are both about devotion,
For which you must be strong, not weak.

For the thinkers, those who live in their heads,
Devotion to knowledge is the way to go.
Through study, and learning – Jnana Yoga -
They will find what they must know.

For the active, those like you and all the rest,
Devotion to work will show the way.
Through pure selfless action – Karma Yoga –
You will be more free each day.

This is your nature, this is your path.
You are a flurry of motion, you do many deeds.
Your body and mind are at work
To fulfill all of your needs.

Use this motion, with the power of will
To control your senses and do your best.
Your work is your duty, and it's also your gift.
Offer this gift to God, and let God do the rest.

Doing work is a reciprocation
For the nourishment that feeds the heart.
Serve God as a way to say "Thank You."
Feed God by doing your part.

When you know who you are,
Then you know you have everything.
You'll know that this work that you do
Is not about gaining anything.

When you work this way,
Unattached to rewards,
There is no effort or strain -
Peace and freedom are yours.

As you know, others are watching you.
Be an example, by doing what's right.
Whatever you do, others will imitate
So, work unattached and shine your light.

Always remember who is the boss,
For the ego will try to get in your way.
Know that it's God moving your limbs;
You aren't the one working anyway.

But I can't make you do anything.
You have a purpose, and you have a choice.
How you live life is all up to you.
This purpose is yours, and so is your voice.

You alone must do what you came here to do.
Do your work and not that of another.
There are duties meant for you in this life,
Don't try to do those meant for your brothers.

ARJUNA:
So, what makes a man,
Even knowing what's right,
Feel compelled to do wrong,
As if he has no might?

KRISHNA:
There's one enemy we can't ignore.
Desire! Its wrath man can't seem to shake.
It's the cause of suffering and sin
In every decision that you make.

Desire is the dust, that keeps shine off the glass.
Desire is the smoke, that blocks out the fire.
You want to know God, to be free, but
What keeps you from Truth is constant desire.

You must be strong to subdue the senses
Drawn to desire – your greatest foe.
Your senses act as a veil hiding your Truth,
Keeping you from seeing the embodied soul.

Desire and its hold can be overcome.
Through work you can lift that veil and see.
The Truth of all life just waiting for you.
Through Karma Yoga you can be free.

Knowledge

यज्ज्ञात्वा न पुनर्मोहमेवं यास्यसि पाण्डव ।
येन भूतान्यशेषेण द्रक्ष्यस्यात्मन्यथो मयि ॥४-३५॥

KRISHNA:
This is the Truth, my friend, and I want you to know it.
You're not my first student, and you won't be my last.
Vivaswat came before you, and he carried the Truth.
His students became teachers and their territory vast.

From teacher to teacher over the years
This knowledge is passed down in a chain.
And when the knowledge is forgotten
I then return to teach again.

ARJUNA:
Vivaswat was born long before you – do the math!
How could you be the first to teach this path?

KRISHNA:
You and I have lived many lives.
You don't remember, you don't recall
The times we've met before this,
But I remember them all.

You know me as I am here,
And it seems that I am born.
But do not trust your senses
And at my death do not mourn.

I am birthless, I am deathless,
Beyond this time and space.
When goodness grows weak on earth,
Then I am needed in this place.

I come to deliver the holy,
To re-establish what is right.
Those who understand my role here
Are guided to the light.

With me you'll find a refuge
From anger, fear, and lust.
I am here to be your safety
And I honor your trust.

Any path that people travel
You'll find will lead to me.
Any prayer that people bring me
You'll find will come to be.

Many turn to worship for
Their own material gain.
Here on earth that is
Easy enough to attain.

But what's the point -
When only more they crave?
They want the fruits and then
To work they are a slave.

Work! Not with results in mind
But liberation – be set free!
And the only way to do that is
To keep your mind on me.

In action there is quietude,
And in quiet so much is done.
Be aware of all you have and are,
Know that we are One.

There is no need to lust or scheme,
There's no need to wear a mask.
The chains you wore are broken
You are up for any task.

There's no jealousy or envy,
No troubles on your mind.
Indifferent to gain or loss,
What you seek you find.

Contentment comes with every gift
No attachments weigh you down.
The illumined heart beats in Brahman
Because Brahman you have found.

Brahman is in every breath,
In every ritual, and every fire.
Brahman is in every step,
And every offering to the fire.

All that you have to offer,
Discipline, work, or study -
All offerings are a sacrifice
Born of action – setting you free.

All action results in Knowledge,
The greatest offering of all.
Pursue the Truth in every way,
Listen and heed the call.

All beings are in your Self
And also in Me.
The Truth clearly shows you this.
Know it and you'll see.

Knowledge shakes you to your core
It transforms your heart.
Seek to obtain Knowledge
Now is the time to start.

With Knowledge comes confidence,
With Knowledge there are no doubts.
Supreme Peace then follows,
As past karma has run out.

Your purpose is to know this Truth,
To cut away delusion.
This Truth is available to all
Who want to see past the illusion.

Arise, O Arjuna!
There is much to do.
Arise, O Arjuna!
See the light within you.

Renunciation

ब्रह्मण्याधाय कर्माणि सङ्गं त्यक्ता करोति यः ।
लिप्यते न स पापेन पद्मपत्रमिवाम्भसा ॥५-१०॥

ARJUNA:
You encourage me to take action –
And say to renounce my every task.
Which am I to do?
O friend, I have to ask.

KRISHNA:
Perform all action rightly and you will be free.
Duty serves a higher purpose than you know.
Renounce all action rightly and you will be free.
Your efforts plant seeds that are destined to grow.

Life is full of opposites
That take us off our course.
We move towards lust or hatred
By an invisible force.

But giving up desire
And letting aversion drop away
Breaks up the cloud of delusion
That colors the sky gray.

Those who do not understand say that
To do and know are two different things.
But the wise see these as one and the same,
Both paths bring clarity.

Take the path that calls to you
And follow it through all its bends.
Seekers meet and find that
In the same freedom both paths end.

It's hard to renounce action
Without taking action first.
Perform your work with devotion
And let Brahman quench your thirst.

When the heart is made pure
And the senses are tamed,
When the body is obedient
And in all Atman is named,

Then as you take action
You'll find no effort spent.
No matter how you move or speak
It's all Brahman that's expressed.

As the lotus rests above the pond
Unwetted by the water,
You'll rise above tempting desire
And know what really matters.

You are not your body,
Nor are you your mind.
Your senses and your intellect
Are tools for use in daily grind.

But you are so much more than this –
Your heart grows full and pure.
United with the Brahman
You find peace forevermore.

Happy is the one who knows
What is true and what is real.
There's no work in any action,
And no suffering to feel.

You can see that any action
Is really but a dream,
And any fruits of all those actions
Are never what they seem.

Brahman, the Lord, is everywhere,
And always by your side.
And yet you remain dreaming,
Asleep with closed eyes.

The Atman, Brahman's light within
Is hidden off and sealed.
But let this sun shine forth and then
The Truth is soon revealed.

The devoted always dwell with Him,
He lives within their heart.
They experience a freedom
From which they never part.

The illumined ones see all the same:
The intellect or fool,
The humble or the boastful,
The elephant or mule.

Absorbed in Brahman,
They see all things as one.
No longer of this world a slave,
For freedom they have won.

The enlightened have a peace of mind
That keeps them calm and balanced.
Unfazed by the good or bad in life,
They remain in Atman's bliss.

Nothing outside sways them
Away from Brahman's joy.
No objects attract the senses,
Toward some trivial toy.

With sins destroyed, and doubts
Dispelled, caring for all beings,
Their lives are changed permanently.
They awaken, clearly seeing.

Meditation

यथा दीपो निवातस्थो नेङ्गते सोपमा स्मृता ।
योगिनो यतचित्तस्य युञ्जतो योगमात्मनः ॥ ६-१९ ॥

KRISHNA:
Those who do their work,
Who set their goal on Me,
Who make no claim to fruits,
These are the true yogis.

But those who avoid the work,
To seek those things outside,
Miss the true serenity
That only abides inside.

You are your own hero.
You are your own best friend.
But you also are your enemy -
Your will is hard to bend.

So, conquer your will
And life will be sublime -
Your heart filled with satisfaction,
Even during the toughest times.

The stone, the earth, the gold –
All from the one place came.
Your well-wishers, friends, and foes –
You'll see are all the same.

You know you must have control
Over the whims of body and mind.
Take some time in solitude
To bask in the Divine.

Meditate upon the Self
Just sit there and be quiet.
This is yoga, union with
The Supreme, that is the Highest.

Sit and hold the body still,
Keep your thoughts on only Me
Then you'll find the peace within
Knowing that One are we.

In all actions maintain a pace,
Never too little or too much.
With moderation in food and sleep
You can lift your sorrows and such.

The yogi with a steady mind,
Serene and concentrated,
Is like the lamp in a windless place
Whose light shines unhesitated.

Experience the boundless joy
Beyond the senses, beyond pain.
There is no greater goal to reach,
No greater peace to gain.

With fortitude and strength of mind,
And in tranquility,
See the world as one in bliss
Because all beings dwell in Me.

When any one of you is suffering,
Feel it as your own, too,
Because we're all connected –
It's "us" not me or you.

ARJUNA:
You make it sound so easy
But my mind's a restless mess.
I can't simply control it –
How? I couldn't even guess.

KRISHNA:
It takes time and it takes practice
To wipe away all doubt.
Just strive to do your best each day
Because all you do does count.

AJUNA:
But what if I can't do it?
What if I should fail?
Then I haven't reached perfection
Nor put wind in my sail.

KRISHNA:
No effort is ever wasted
All you do is for your good.
And one day you'll understand this,
As I've always said you would.

It might be in this lifetime
Or it may be in another.
Our journeys may be different
But we all are joined in Mother.

Worship then, with faith and love,
Steadfast, along with Me.
Practice with all your heart in it –
Illusions fade, and then you'll see.

Chapter

7

Realization

मत्तः परतरं नान्यत्किं चिदस्ति धनंजय ।
मयि सर्वमिदं प्रोतं सूत्रे मणिगणा इव ॥ ७-७॥

KRISHNA:
Hear Me. Find your answers in Me.
Let your mind attach to Me and you will Know Me.

Take in this knowledge – as you bloom and grow.
Paired with experience, there's nothing more for you to know.

Among thousands of beings here on this earth, just one might look for Me.
And just one of those, of all of those, might the Truth see.

I am everywhere – in the earth and in the fire and the air. You'll find
I am water, and I am space – your intellect, and ego, and your mind.

I am all of Nature, it is true. But there is so much more to me than this.
I am the Indwelling Spirit that sustains the universe and All That Is.

Think of Me as a thread, on which all the blessings of the world are strung.
Like pearls on a strand, you'll see that together we are all One.

The sun's radiance is Me, and I am the mighty Om.
Wherever you go, I am with you and you are home.

I am the sweet fragrance in the earth and I am what makes fire bright.
I am the Eternal Seed of all that lives, and in all beings I am life.

This world is a messy place – filled with moods and mental states.
These expressions come from me, but I am not in them, don't take the bait.

When you look at these distractions, you fail to see me as I am.
Look past the illusions, break through the veil of Maya if you can.

Delusions hold you hostage, deprived of knowledge, never free.
Turn away from all that blinds you, seek the Truth and you'll find Me.

There are four types of people who follow me – first, the person in distress.
Then the person seeking knowledge, and then the one seeking some rest.

But then there's the one with wisdom, devoted and steadfast.
To this one knowledge comes easily and lasts.

It takes many lifetimes for one to be so wise.
And they shall surely be Self-realized.

Worship is not something with which you should play,
To fulfill the desires that have led you astray.

Those with small minds sense the finite and want more –
They think that I am in a manifest form.

To those who see only Maya I am not revealed.
They don't know what they're missing, they don't know what is real.

But I can see all, and I know how it goes.
This spell they are under is the cause of their woes.

From the time one arrives, from the moment of birth,
Desire and aversion tie you to this earth.

But there are those who do virtuous deeds,
Freed from delusion, they have simple needs.

From karma and fear there's no other release;
United with Brahman, you'll find bliss and peace.

The Way to Brahman

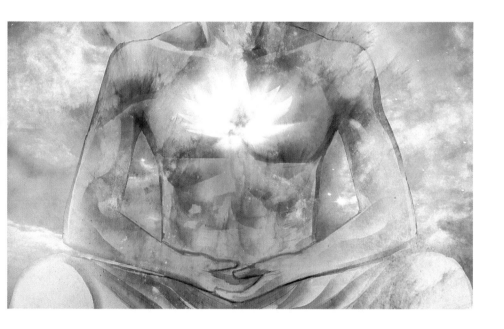

सर्वद्वाराणि संयम्य मनो हृदि निरुध्य च ।
मूर्ध्न्याधायात्मनः प्राणमास्थितो योगधारणाम् ॥८-१२॥

ARJUNA:
Just what is Brahman? Help me understand.
What is the soul, what gives us breath?
And even if we practice self-control,
How are we to know You at our death?

KRISHNA:
Brahman is the Imperishable,
Brahman is the Supreme.
Brahman is your individual soul –
Heaven, earth and all that's in between.

Anything made up of the elements,
All matter you can see, taste, or feel –
All of it is perishable.
It doesn't last – it's all "unreal."

Yet behind all things, all actions that take place
Is a Cosmic Spirit that never dies.
It is ancient and it is unborn –
It is the Brahman that in all things resides.

When it's time to leave your body
Remember Me, just think of my name.
And you will merge with Brahman.
What you think of, you will surely attain.

At all times, always remember Me.
Absorb Me with your mind and understanding.
Filled with love, and armed with strength, radiant
As light, reach Brahman by meditating.

You all have access to Me always. Just close
The door of the senses and be still.
Say the mantra "Om" denoting Brahman
And as a lotus opens, your heart fills.

The dwellers in the world have all been here before,
And to this world will be reborn again.
But those who reach Me, the Illumined ones,
Are free from what is transient, free from pain.

The wise know that to the one who creates
A thousand ages is merely a day.
And night is then a thousand ages more.
In Spirit there is no time and space.

To go from one life to another is
Like sleeping and then becoming awake.
In sleep, there's no awareness of the body
As if in an unmanifested state.

Beyond this state is the Imperishable,
The Ultimate Goal, My Supreme Abode.
Pervaded through all the worlds, accessed by
Whole-souled devotion to God alone.

Those who don't want to be reborn anymore
Meet the lighted path when the moon is bright.
And those who must still return here again,
Take the path of smoke and dark of night.

You can study the scriptures and give alms,
Sacrifice and practice austerities.
But heed my teaching and meditate,
And illumined you will certainly be.

Mystery

तपाम्यहमहं वर्षं निगृह्णाम्युत्सृजामि च ।
अमृतं चैव मृत्युश्च सदसच्चाहमर्जुन ॥९-१९॥

Because you accept me,
And I see you trust me –
Let me share this secret
Of what it is that could be.

Knowledge of God,
Nearer than knowing,
A vision so clear,
Direct and flowing

Unties the binds
From dying and birth.
Understand this and
Be free of this earth.

This is the king of secrets,
The knowledge most high,
Only made plain
In the mystic's eye.

This secret has virtue,
This secret is pure.
The truth of this secret
Is eternal and sure.

This entire universe
Rests in my infinite form.
I sustain every creature,
Even the unborn.

How this could ever be
Is my divine mystery.
As all air remains in space
All of life lives within me.

Those without faith in Me,
Or faith in My words,
Shall fail to find Me
And return to this world.

For these helpless ones,
Oh, Maya is king!
They attach to illusion
Instead of awakening.

And I just watch as
Maya casts its spell,
Creating distractions
That they think are real.

Yet I am right here
And they do not see,
The Lord, and their soul,
In its majesty.

I am the master of Maya
That makes all things,
That keeps the world turning
And destroys all things.

But fools pass by blindly,
They know nothing at all.
Bewildered and vain,
Into madness they fall.

Then there are those great in soul
Who strive to be good and be kind.
They do good works
With unwavering minds.

Their hearts full of love
And lips giving praise,
They worship with faith -
No doubts do they raise.

Some know Brahman in all things,
And some see us as one in all places.
Others bow to the many gods
That are my million faces.

I am also the Vedas,
The rituals and rites.
I am the food and the herbs.
I am the path and I am the light.

I am the offering
And I am the fire,
I am the sun's heat
And also its sire.

I am the beginning
And the place you call home.
I am the friend and the
Refuge, I am the OM.

I let loose the rain,
And I also withhold it.
I am the cosmos revealed
And all who behold it.

They who are versed in
The scriptures and rites,
Pray for passage to heaven
And celestial delights.

And they're granted this wish
They attain Indra's sphere,
Till they exhaust their merit
And return again here.

Still hungry for more,
With desires burning,
They're drawn by the senses
To endless returning.

The ones who will worship
And meditate on me,
With minds undistracted
I supply all of their needs.

Worship a deity and
Them you will go to.
Ancestors, elements,
Or spirits can draw you.

But this is still a
Mistaken approach.
By not knowing Me
You're missing the boat.

I am the only
One who receives
Your offers or prayers
So come straight to Me.

Whatever your action,
Whatever your gift,
I will accept it
And your heart uplift.

All that you do to
Help one another
You do for Me,
There are no others.

It doesn't matter to Me
How awful your sins.
When you show me devotion
Holiness begins.

United with me
You are set free from karma.
Come into my Being,
This is your dharma.

The Divine

यद्यद्विभूतिमत्सत्त्वं श्रीमदूर्जितमेव वा ।
तत्तदेवावगच्छ त्वं मम तेजोंऽशसंभवम् ॥ १०-४१ ॥

KRISHNA:
Mighty warrior, dear friend,
I care about your welfare.
You delight in my wisdom,
So, I impart these words so rare.

The devas, the gods, the sages –
Don't know from where I came.
How could they? I am their source,
The sustainer of all you name.

Those who know Me as birthless,
With no beginning and no end –
Those undeluded mortals
Shall be forever freed from sin.

All attributes of all beings
Arise from Me alone:
Forbearance, fear, and power,
Pleasure and self-control.

All of the world's creatures
Have sprung from my roots.
Those who dwell in my yoga
Are certain of this Truth.

The wise know that I am
The origin of all.
With their life absorbed in Me
Their devotion never stalls.

I, out of compassion,
Dwelling in their hearts,
Light the lamp of wisdom
That obliterates the dark.

ARJUNA:
Your words to me are sacred
They fill my heart with delight.
How can I become illumined?
I want to bask in your light.

You are the Supreme Brahman
As others have proclaimed.
How can I best know You?
Please tell me – explain.

KRISHNA:
My divine attributes are many
There is no limit to my extent.
To share some preeminent ones
With you, that is my intent.

I am the Self of each creature,
Seated in their hearts.
This is how you can see Me,
Why we can never be apart.

I am manifested in all things,
Through which I come to be.
Look to the highest and the best
And Divinity you'll see.

Of the Adityas I am Vishnu;
Of all the lights I am the sun.
Of the birds I am Garuda,
Of the beasts I am the lion.

Of the rivers I am the Ganges,
Of the fish I am the shark.
Of the water I am the ocean.
Of men I am the monarch.

Of words I am the OM,
And of the Vasus I am fire.
Of mountains I am Meru.
I am inexhaustible Time.

I am the vigor of the strong
And I am also victory.
I am Glory, Speech, Forbearance,
Fortune and Memory.

Of purifiers I am the wind,
And of seasons I am the spring.
And in disputations
I am clear reasoning,

Of secrets I am silence,
I am the wisdom of the wise.
I am the seed of all that exists,
In every color, shape and size.

Whatever glorious or beautiful
Or mighty that you see,
Know that it has sprung from
But a spark from Me.

This is just a sample of
My splendor, put into words.
With a single fragment of Myself
I support the whole universe.

The Vision

किरीटिनं गदिनं चक्रिणं च
तेजोराशिं सर्वतो दीप्तिमन्तम् ।
पश्यामि त्वां दुर्निरीक्ष्यं समन्ताद्
दीप्तानलार्कद्युतिमप्रमेयम् ॥११-१७॥

ARJUNA:
With compassion You have taught me
And I know You are so wise.
I have learned so much about You,
Yet I want to see this with my own eyes.

O Lord, if You think me able
To behold it, please reveal
Your Immutable Self, the Divine,
Your omniscience, the Ideal.

KRISHNA:
Look around you and you see
All the amazing forms of Me.
The whole universe is held
Within my very body.

But with your human eyes
You cannot take it all in.
I give you a divine eye,
So you may see within.

ARJUNA:
O Lord, in Your body,
All that I behold!
All the god and goddesses –
All the diverse beings in your fold.

Myriads of arms and bellies,
With myriads of faces and eyes!
I behold You as Universal,
Infinite on every side.

I behold You on all sides, glowing
Radiant like a fire,
Blazing like the burning sun!
My eyes shrink from Your splendor.

By You alone is filled all
The space between Heaven and Earth,
And all the quarters of the sky.
All three worlds behold your girth.

Bands of Rishis and Siddhas
Praise You with splendid hymns.
Of Your brilliance some are frightened
Yet Your brightness never dims.

I behold Your mouths, striking
Terror with their sharp teeth -
Please be gracious, O Lord
For I am scared and find no peace.

As the many torrents of
The rivers rush toward the sea,
The heroes of the world
Fiercely rush into Thee.

As moths rush into a flame
And there they meet their death,
These creatures rush to Your mouth
Where they take their final breath.

You devour all the worlds.
Have mercy upon me!
I want to understand why -
I desire to know Thee.

KRISHNA:
I am world-destroying Time,
Now engaged slaying these men.
Even without you or war
All warriors shall meet their end.

So, stand up and win glory;
Win your kingdom, seem to slay.
By Me and none other,
They will die anyway.

Kill your enemies in this fight.
They've already been killed by Me.
Be not distressed by fear,
You shall conquer, you will see.

ARJUNA:
O Krishna, the world rejoices
In glorifying Thee.
And why should they not? You are
Being and non-being.

You are the ancient Soul,
The supreme Resting place.
You are the Knower and the known,
Pervading infinite space.

Salutations to You
A Thousand times, and more!
You pervade all the world
And You are all therefore.

Carelessly I've addressed You,
As my comrade, or my friend,
I didn't know Your greatness.
Please forgive me, down I bend.

You are the world's Father and
The object of its praise.
You are its greatest Teacher,
Supreme in every way.

Dear Lord, I bow before You
And humbly seek Your grace.
I rejoice and I am grateful
To have seen Your perfect face.

But my mind is also troubled,
I'm trembling with fear.
I beg to see your human form
Again, that I hold dear.

KRISHNA:
By My grace and through My power
You've witnessed my form Supreme -
Infinite, resplendent,
A sight none has ever seen.

And neither by study,
Nor by rituals or gifts,
Will anyone but you
See Me into this form shift.

So, be not bewildered
By this terrific form of Mine.
Free from fear, glad at heart,
Behold My familiar design.

ARJUNA:
Seeing You as human,
So gentle and so kind,
I feel like myself again,
I have composed my mind.

KRISHNA:
Only by devotion
May my true form be known
To those who do My work
And through whom love is shown.

Devotion

अद्वेष्टा सर्वभूतानां मैत्रः करुण एव च ।
निर्ममो निरहंकारः समदुःखसुखः क्षमी ॥ १२-१३ ॥

ARJUNA:
Some worship You with devotion,
Some worship God, the Unmanifest.
Who, between these two, has the
Understanding of You that is best?

KRISHNA:
Those whose minds are fixed on Me
With absolute faith and pure love,
Have a deep perception of yoga,
They know what the world is made of.

As for those who control their senses,
And are devoted to humanity,
They see Atman in every creature,
And they certainly will come to Me.

But those who embrace the Unmanifest -
Have a difficult task to finalize,
As having an embodied soul makes
The Unmanifest hard to realize.

I come quickly to those who offer
Every action and prayer to Me.
Because they love Me I shall save them,
From the waves of Life's deathly sea.

Rest your thoughts on Me in concentration.
Absorbed in Me thus, there you shall dwell.
Do not doubt it, here and hereafter
The mind is tranquil and all is well.

If concentration in Me eludes you,
Then practice through meditation.
And if you lack the strength to do this,
Reach Me through pure devotion.

And if you are unable to do this
Then surrender yourself completely.
Give up all of the fruits of your actions
And devote all of your work to Me.

Concentration practiced with discernment
Is better than rituals unceased.
Absorption in God is even better,
And renunciation brings instant peace.

Be friendly to all living beings.
Show compassion to everyone.
Be free from delusions of "I" and "mine."
Accept pleasure and pain as if one.

Be forgiving and ever contented.
Be united with Me constantly.
Your resolve must never be shaken.
Such a devotee is dear to Me.

Be pure, free from the body's desires.
Unbothered, prepared for anything,
Be unmoved by good or bad fortune.
Such a devotee is dear to Me.

Untroubled, renounce all undertakings.
Be indifferent to cold or to heat.
Remain unchanged by praise and by blame,
Such a devotee is dear to Me.

The seekers who practice this wisdom
Will be led to immortality.
All those who see me as the Supreme Goal -
These devotees are dearest to Me.

The Field and Its Knower

महाभूतान्यहंकारो बुद्धिरव्यक्तमेव च ।
इन्द्रियाणि दशैकं च पञ्च चेन्द्रियगोचराः ॥१३-५॥

ARJUNA:
All around is matter, called nature –
And it is also called the Field.
And I know there's also Spirit,
Which is the Knower of the Field.

How does this relate to knowledge
And that which is to be known?
I want so much to understand this.
I want so dearly to be shown.

KRISHNA:
Take a look at your strong body,
It's an example of the Field.
And he who knows this body,
Is the Knower of the Field.

In this Field you sow seeds of action,
And in this Field you reap their fruits.
The wise say that this Field's Knower
Is the one who watches from its roots.

To discern between Field and Knower
Is knowledge of the highest kind.
And know that I am the Knower
Of all the Fields you'll ever find.

Now listen closely I will tell you
About this Field and whence it comes.
I will tell you of its Knower,
And the powers of this One.

All this has been sung by sages
In many ways and different hymns,
And in well-reasoned passages
On the nature of Brahman.

What is this Field made of?
Is this mere body what it seems?
You are nature in the cosmos
All that is seen and still unseen.

The great elements compose you,
Earth, water, fire, space and air.
Also, intellect, mind, and ego,
Senses and sense-objects they share.

Ten organs of knowing and doing,
Desire, hatred, pleasure and pain,
Fortitude and resolution,
Plus the Spirit that remains.

The Field has limits and it changes,
So be careful with what you do.
Be humble, harmless, and helpful.
Be tranquil, steadfast, and true.

Don't be a slave to your senses.
Keep your weaknesses in mind.
The body ages and it suffers
And it eventually dies.

Have no desire for possessions.
Be calm in any circumstance.
Be upright and forbearing,
And practice cleanliness.

With your heart undistracted,
Turn your thoughts toward solitude.
Seek the knowledge of the Atman
And know why this you should do.

Those who practice these attributes
Are led to great wisdom.
It's only ignorance then,
That could ever deny them.

Now I'll describe That which must be known
In order to gain immortality.
Eternal Brahman, beginningless, is
Beyond what is, and is not, equally.

Brahman's hands and feet are everywhere,
As are its eyes and heads and faces.
Its ears are everywhere in the world.
Its existence is in all places.

It shines through the senses doing their tasks
Yet Itself of senses is devoid.
It is devoid of preferences and yet
All experiences It enjoys.

It is without and within all beings.
Brahman is moving and also at rest.
Incomprehensible, and subtle.
Brahman is far and also nearest.

Indivisible, and yet divided
Amongst all beings in all nature,
Knowable Brahman, Sustainer of all,
Is yet the Creator and Destroyer.

Brahman is the Light even of lights.
As knowledge, its object and its Goal,
Brahman is beyond any darkness,
It is set firm in the hearts of all.

That's the Field, knowledge, and its object.
Devotees who understand this
Become worthy of My divine state
And experience divine bliss.

Nature and soul have no beginning.
All forms and tendencies come from Nature.
Nature is said to be the cause
Of the body of every creature.

Spirit, embodied in Nature,
Reflects tendencies from which it is born.
Attachment to these tendencies
Causes the birth into which it is born.

Brahman in the body is the one
Highest Self, Witness, and Supporter.
Knowing Nature, Spirit and tendencies
May express through but is not again born.

Some meditate to perceive this High Self.
Some feel it through dedication to work.
And some who are curious find
Through diligence to knowledge its spark.

And yet there are some who don't use these means.
They know the Divine from devotion.
They pass beyond death from what they have heard
And the holy words that are spoken.

Everything born, that moves or does not,
Is the Field and its Knower united.
Those who see Brahman alike in all,
Not perishing, He alone is sighted.

Because he sees the Lord everywhere,
He does not injure anything.
And thus by his acts of compassion
He then reaches the state supreme.

Those who know that all actions are done
By nature and its tendencies,
That Spirit is merely the witness,
Verily, he alone sees.

Those who see that the manifold nature
Of all beings is centered in the One,
That evolution comes from that alone,
Those devotees become one with Brahman.

This supreme, imperishable Self
With no beginning, and no tendencies,
Neither acts, nor is stained by action
Even while dwelling in the body.

Space that pervades all things is subtle,
And it cannot ever be stained,
So the Self dwelling in the body
Everywhere also cannot be stained.

As the one sun illumines this world,
The Brahman illumines the body.
As the one sun illumines this world,
The Brahman illumines all bodies.

Those who know the Knower from its Field
And how we can arise above our nature
That is the cause of all beings,
They attain My Supreme favor.

Human Tendencies

समदुःखसुखः स्वस्थः समलोष्टाश्मकाञ्चनः ।
तुल्यप्रियाप्रियो धीरस्तुल्यनिन्दात्मसंस्तुतिः ॥१४-२४॥

KRISHNA:
The Supreme Knowledge I share with you.
The sages with this understanding gained,
After passing from this world,
The highest perfection have attained.

Made one with my holy nature
Now they are free and not reborn.
And they have no fear of dying
When the body is outworn.

The Great Nature is My womb.
I am the Father of all things.
And it is this womb of Nature
From which every creature springs.

From this Nature come the gunas,
You could call them human tendencies.
These are the bonds that bind you
Imprisoning you in your body.

The first guna is called Sattva.
You'll know it by its pure light.
Yet even sattva will bind you
To search for knowledge and delight.

The guna Rajas is impulsive.
It is all about the passion.
Whether pleasure or possession,
It makes you hungry for action.

The guna Tamas makes you lazy,
Binding you with delusion.
Tamas is born of ignorance,
Bringing dullness and confusion.

Sattva enslaves you to happiness.
And Rajas enslaves you to take action.
And Tamas enslaves the deluded
And darkens their every decision.

The guna that is the strongest
Prevails over the other two.
Be ever mindful of which guna
Has its influence over you.

When understanding shines through the body
Sattva is present and has prevailed.
When greed, unrest, and longing arise,
Then you know Rajas has prevailed.

And when inertia takes over
With its darkness and lethargy,
When incompetence is dominant,
You know it's the Tamas tendency.

If the embodied soul meets with death
And sattva has shone the brightest,
It finds the realm known as heaven
For those who know the Highest.

If a soul meets with death filled with rajas
It returns to those attached to action.
If a soul meets with death filled with tamas
It returns to those devoid of reason.

The fruit of sattva is good and clean.
But the fruit of rajas is pain.
And the fruit of tamas is ignorance.
Always keep your tendencies on reins.

Those established in sattva go upward.
Those who are moved by rajas stay the same.
And those who are steeped in tamas,
Heavy, they move downward in the game.

The wise know the gunas as the doers
Of every action and attitude,
Let them learn to know That which is beyond
And with My oneness to attune.

ARJUNA:
How can we rise above the gunas?
What does such a man look like?
How will I know when I have gotten there?
What will my behavior be like?

KRISHNA:
One who has transcended the gunas
Hates not, nor longs for anything.
Unconcerned, unmoved by the gunas,
Calm in happiness, or suffering.

He sees all things as of equal value,
Whether stone, earth, or a piece of gold.
Alike in pleasure or pain, he is
No different whether praised or scolded.

The same in honor and dishonor,
He is the same to friend and to foe.
He who has renounced all undertakings,
He has above the gunas rose.

He who worships Me with steadfast love,
Rises above the gunas to be free.
I am the Abode of Brahman,
Truth, bliss, and life immortal, come to Me.

The Tree

श्रीभगवानुवाच ।

ऊर्ध्वमूलमधःशाखमश्वत्थं प्राहुरव्ययम् ।

छन्दांसि यस्य पर्णानि यस्तं वेद स वेदवित् ॥ १५-१ ॥

KRISHNA:
The scriptures talk of an ancient tree,
The giant Asvattha never ages.
Rooted in heaven with branches below,
Each leaf sings a song of the Vedas.

Those who know of this special tree
Are availed of the Vedas insights.
Above and below spread its branches,
Fed by the gunas day and night.

Its buds are the things of the senses -
The physical means of attraction.
Its roots reach down to the world of men
Becoming the roots of man's action.

Its true form is not comprehended,
Nor its existence, or its intent.
But with Brahman in your contemplation
You sharpen the axe of detachment.

With the sharp axe of detachment
Cut through this firmly-rooted tree.
Seek the Goal from which you don't return,
The source of eternal activity.

Once freed from pride and delusion,
No pawn for attachment's hold,
Desires stilled, calm in pleasure and pain,
You have reached that Immutable Goal.

This is my Infinite Being,
With no need for the light of the sun,
It shines Self-luminous always.
Reach me and never be reborn.

Part of Me is the God within you,
And every living creature you'll find.
The soul eternal, seeming separate,
Wearing nature's body and mind.

When the Lord puts on a body,
Or when the body He removes,
The mind and senses go with Him,
As the wind takes the flower's perfume.

Presiding over the ear and eye,
Touch, taste, smell, and also the mind,
He enjoys and suffers all the things
Of the senses with all mankind.

The deluded do not perceive him
In the body or when he departs,
Nor in the gunas or motions.
But the sages see him with the heart.

Those who are practiced and tranquil
Behold him dwelling within.
But there are those who don't find him.
They may try, though they are undisciplined.

The light that is in the sun and the moon,
And likewise is in the fire,
Illuminating the whole universe,
This light is from Me acquired.

My energy here on the earth
Sustains all living beings.
I'm the moon, giving water and sap
To feed all the plants and the trees.

As the flame of life in all beings
I digest the foods that you eat,
Providing strength for the body
And energy for each heartbeat.

I am in every creature's heart.
Your knowledge and memory,
I both give and take away.
All of Vedanta is from Me.

Two parts of existence make up this world:
The mortal and the immortal.
All creatures are mortal through our eyes.
And God, the Unchanging, is immortal.

But there is one other than these,
The Highest, the Atman, Supreme.
The Unchanging Lord, pervading all worlds,
Sustains and supports everything.

I am known in this world and the Vedas
As the Supreme Reality.
This sacred truth I have taught you.
Know this truth and wise you will be.

The Divine and The Demonic

तस्माच्छास्त्रं प्रमाणं ते कार्याकार्यव्यवस्थितौ ।
ज्ञात्वा शास्त्रविधानोक्तं कर्म कर्तुमिहार्हसि ॥१६-२४॥

KRISHNA:

Fearlessness, purity of heart,
Self-control, sacrifice, and charity,
Steadfast study of the scriptures,
Uprightness, and austerity.

Gentleness, truth, and loyalty,
Tranquility, freedom from anger,
Renunciation, compassion,
Modesty, aversion to slander.

Courage, forgiveness, fortitude,
Abstained from useless activity,
Faith in strength and fortitude,
Thoughts and actions all purity.

These are the qualities of one
Born to move toward the Divine.
Work to cultivate these qualities
And divine treasures you will find.

When born with demonic tendencies,
Arrogance, anger and conceit,
One is bound to live in ignorance,
In bondage, and in defeat.

The divine treasures have a purpose,
They are tools to set one free.
Demonic traits keep those imprisoned.
You, friend, move towards divinity.

There are two types of beings in this world,
The demonic and divine both live here.
I've explained a lot of the divine,
Now about the demonic lend an ear.

Those of demonic nature know not
What to do or from what to refrain.
There is no purity in them,
No good conduct, and no restraint.

These people are devoid of morals,
They say the world is without a God.
Made by the merging of two genders,
They say that lust is its real cause.

Lost souls, with little understanding,
Tricked by the darkness in their minds,
They act out to destroy the world, they are
The enemies of all mankind.

Filled with hypocrisy and pride,
Their lust can never be appeased.
Busy satiating their greed,
The ends they work for are unclean.

Plagued by fear and anxiety
They strive for gratification
Of their desires, their highest goal,
Unaware of the fear's causation.

Amassing wealth, they're pleasure addicts,
Working to satisfy their passions,
Bound to this world with golden chains,
To keep up with the latest fashions.

They say: "I have gained this, and that I want,
This wealth and that shall be mine.
I've slain my foe, and others, too
I'm having a marvelous time."

They offer sacrifices
Which are so only in name,
When they give anything at all
They give it expecting fame.

Self-honored and haughty
Intoxicated by wealth,
Weighted by ego and pride,
They fall into a loathsome hell.

These cruel haters and evil-doers,
Are ruined by lust, wrath, and greed.
These three gates of hell men must renounce
Or never will they attain Me.

One who escapes these three gates so dark,
And virtuous qualities extols,
Knows what is good for himself and the world
And thus attains the Supreme Goal.

One who discards the words of the scripture,
And impulsively pursues desire,
Attains neither perfection, nor joy,
Nor the Supreme Goal acquire.

In deciding what you must do,
And from which you must abstain,
Let the scriptures be your guide,
And do your work that pertains.

Three Kinds of Faith

अश्रद्धया हुतं दत्तं तपस्तप्तं कृतं च यत् ।
असदित्युच्यते पार्थ न च तत्प्रेत्य नो इह ॥१७-२८॥

ARJUNA:
There are those who sacrifice to God
With true faith and devotion,
But what kind of faith would also
Discard the scriptures injunctions?

KRISHNA:
With humans there are three kinds of faith
Based on each personality.
Sattva, rajas, or tamas, will
Correspond individually.

Those who are dominant in sattva
Worship God in the many aspects.
Rajasic ones worship power.
The tamasic worship ghosts in respect.

The vain ones of demonic nature,
Impelled by the force of lust and greed,
Subject the body to torture
And also hurt the one within – Me.

Food is also of the three kinds,
As are sacrifices and gifts.
Listen – I'll explain the difference
And then your thinking will shift.

Food that is succulent and healthy,
Giving appetite, and vitality,
Is favored by those endowed with sattva.
This food gives them longevity.

Food that's too bitter, sour, salty,
Burning that brings you to your knees,
Is liked by those endowed with rajas,
Though it causes pain, grief, and disease.

Food that is stale and tasteless,
Putrid, unclean or rotten
Is liked by those endowed with tamas,
Health for them is misbegotten.

And when it comes to sacrifice
The sattvic expect no reward.
They offer according to scripture
This is a duty they look toward.

Those with the nature of rajas
Sacrifice with much expectation.
They perform for the rewards and
For the sake of ostentation.

Those with the nature of tamas
Offer no food, and chant no hymns.
They feel no need to give money,
If there's any faith it's very dim.

Austerity of the body
Means reverence for teachers and the wise.
Cleanliness, continence, harmlessness,
Are virtues the scriptures advise.

Practice austerity of speech
With words that are pleasant and truthful.
Recitation of the Vedas
Is also very beneficial.

Practice austerity of the mind
With silence and serenity.
With gentleness and self-control
The heart is filled with purity.

This threefold austerity
Practiced with faith and devotion,
With no desire for reward
Is sattvic in nature and golden.

But when practiced to gain respect
Or honor, or merely for show
This is of the nature of rajas
Its result is uncertain with no flow.

When austerity is practiced
With some foolish purpose, or for harm
This is the nature of tamas
It is dark, dull and without charm.

A gift made to one deserving,
At the right time and the right place
With no strings attached or hoped-for,
This is sattva shining its grace.

A gift offered with reluctance
Or expectation of recompense
Is seeped in the nature of rajas -
The motives are from selfishness.

A gift made to one unworthy
Offered without respect, or with disdain,
Is dense with the nature of tamas
And no regard does it contain.

Om Tat Sat: Three words designate Brahman,
By which all of creation arose,
The Vedas, sacrifices, and seers
In ancient times, and so it goes.

Therefore OM is always the first word
Said by a Brahman devotee
With any act of sacrifice,
Or a gift, or austerity.

And TAT, meaning the Absolute,
Is said without expectations,
With sacrifices, gifts and more
By those seeking liberation.

And SAT, goodness and existence,
Also means steadfastness in faith.
This word is used in connection
With auspicious action you take.

With any act of sacrifice,
With any gift or austerity
Direct your faith and will towards Brahman.
Without faith, there's no prosperity.

Liberation

तमेव शरणं गच्छ सर्वभावेन भारत ।
तत्प्रसादात्परां शान्तिं स्थानं प्राप्स्यसि शाश्वतम् ॥१८-६२॥

ARJUNA:
Tell me about renunciation,
I want to learn the truth -
And about nonattachment,
And the different between the two.

KRISHNA:
The sages say renunciation is
Giving up actions driven by desire
And nonattachment means
Not working for the fruit acquired.

Some say all actions should be dropped
As they might be seen as immoral.
And acts of sacrifice, austerity,
And gifts are the only acts moral.

Now you shall hear the truth from Me
About relinquishment,
Declared to be of three kinds.
Pay attention and be diligent.

Sacrifice, gifts and austerity
Must be performed, not resigned.
These means of purification
Are provided for the wise.

Even these good works though
Must be done without attachment
Or desire for any fruits.
This is my considered judgment.

Renunciation, out of ignorance,
Of the actions the scriptures ordain
Is of the nature of tamas
And is not proper to attain.

Renunciation of a duty,
From fear of suffering or pain
Is of the nature of rajas -
There are no benefits to obtain.

Perform an obligatory action
Only because it should be done.
Renounce all attachments and the fruit,
And sattva shines through like the sun.

A wise one does not shrink from doing
What may be seen as disagreeable.
Nor does one feel any attachment
To a duty seen as agreeable.

No one can renounce action completely.
But when one is from the fruits detached
And does the work well anyway,
That one is said to be nonattached.

To those who are centered in the ego,
Action brings three kinds of fruits:
The pleasant, unpleasant, or mixed.
But they are free who give ego the boot.

Five causes bring about achievement
As declared in high philosophy.
The body, the doer, and the senses,
The breath and the presiding deity.

Whatever action is performed,
With the body, speech or mind,
Whether right or whether wrong,
The cause of it comes from these five.

The one who misunderstands this
And thinks he hasn't any fault
Is of a confused mind
And does not see at all.

But the one untainted by ego,
Whose understanding is clear,
Though he slays thousands he slays not,
To no action does he adhere.

There are three incitements to action:
Knowledge, its object and the knower.
And the threefold basis of action:
The instrument, the object, the doer.

Knowledge, action and the doer,
Philosophy says are of three kinds.
Each one has its own distinction,
Each one is with a guna aligned.

The knowledge of one eternal Substance
Seen in every being everywhere,
Undivided in the divided,
This is sattva knowledge declared.

The knowledge that sees us all as separate,
Different entities of different types,
This is the nature of rajas
That sees us as each unalike.

The knowledge that see one single
Event as if it were the whole
Is without reason or foundation
This is where tamas plays its role.

An obligatory action
Done by one without hate or love,
Unattached, and wanting no fruit,
This is sattvic action thereof.

The action performed with much effort,
By one with desires to gratify,
That action comes from rajas,
Prompted by a feeling of "I."

An action taken through ignorance,
Without regard to injury,
Is an action steeped in tamas
With no view of one's ability.

The doer free from attachment,
Endowed with fortitude and zeal,
Unmoved by success or failure,
Is full of sattva, the real deal.

The doer attached to action,
Who is greedy, violent, and impure,
Struck down in sorrow, elated by joy,
Has rajasic nature, that's for sure.

The doer who is apathetic,
Deceitful, malicious, and despondent,
Who always tries to procrastinate,
The tamasic nature represents.

Now let's talk of understanding
And the three distinctions that apply.
This also goes for determination.
Each one I'll explain and certify.

One who knows right from wrong action,
Who turns away from worldly desire,
Who accepts and strives for liberation,
In this one sattva has transpired.

One who cannot discern truly or
Know what should and should not be done,
Has a distorted understanding.
In this one rajas has overcome.

One who is wrapped in ignorance,
Often mistaking wrong for right,
Reverses all the values and
Is stuck in a dark tamasic blight.

Firmness that comes with concentration
Allows for perfect self-control
Of the mind, energy and senses.
In this one it's sattva that's bestowed.

Determined to get pleasure and wealth,
Desirous of the fruits of each,
Working with intense attachment,
Onto this one rajas has leeched.

One stubborn with his fear and grief,
Craving sleep and sensuality,
Determined to take no action,
Of tamasic nature he must be.

There are also three kinds of happiness.
One that comes from joy in practice,
Poison at first, yet nectar in the end.
From self-knowledge, is sattva active.

The joy stimulated by objects
And the senses with which they connect,
Nectar at first, but poison in the end,
Comes from the rajasic effect.

That which springs from sleep, sloth and error,
Deluding the soul from start to end
Has all the nature of tamas and
Its brutish contentment defends.

The gunas affect every creature
We cannot escape their influence
As long as we live in this body
Their presence is continuous.

We each are given a purpose
A dharma, a duty of our own.
Be devoted to this dharma
By which your true Self will be known.

Worship Him from whom all arise,
Who fills the universe to the brim,
Through duty one attains perfection,
Through duty one worships Him.

Do your dharma, though imperfect,
Not the dharma of another well.
Your dharma is your duty
Through it your knowledge swells.

Don't give up on your duty,
Though you may see it as broke.
All duties are imperfect
Just as fire is beset with smoke.

With mind unattached to anything,
Renounce, and attain perfection.
With heart subdued, free from longing,
This is freedom from all action.

Learn from me, O Arjuna,
How one who has reached such perfection
Realizes Brahman, which is
Of knowledge, the supreme consummation.

Endowed with pure understanding,
Restraining with determination,
Turning away from senses and objects,
Shunning attachment and revulsion;

Abiding in solitude, self-control,
Ever engaged in meditation,
Cultivating freedom from passion,
Exercising concentration;

Forsaking conceit and power,
Pride and lust, wrath and property,
Tranquil in heart, and free from ego,
To be one with Brahman, he is worthy.

As Brahman, and tranquil in heart,
This one neither desires nor grieves.
He treats all beings alike, and
Attains supreme devotion to Me.

By that devotion he knows Me,
Knows what, in truth, I am and who.
Then he forthwith enters into Me,
Having known Me in truth.

Even though engaged in actions,
One who has taken refuge in Me,
By My grace reaches the eternal
And imperishable Dwelling.

Regarding Me as the Supreme Goal,
Surrendering, in thought, all activity,
Practicing steadiness of mind,
Fix your heart constantly on Me.

With your heart fixed on Me, you will
Overcome every difficulty.
But if you choose not to listen
You shall perish utterly.

If, indulging in self-conceit,
"I will not fight," to yourself you say,
Vain is your resolution.
Your very nature will obligate.

Bound by your own karma,
Which of your own nature evolved,
What through delusion you seek not to do,
You shall do, even against your resolve.

O Arjuna, this you should know:
The Lord lives in the hearts of all beings.
He turns them around as if in play
On the wheel of his maya machine.

Take refuge in Him with all your soul,
By His grace will you gain Supreme Peace.
Thus has profound wisdom been declared
To you, my dear friend, by Me.

Reflect upon all this fully,
You must decide what you will do.
You are well beloved of Me,
I want what is for your good, too.

With your whole heart, devoted to Me,
You shall find Me, I promise you.
Lay down your duties in me, your refuge.
From all sin I will deliver you.

You must not speak this holy truth to one
Lacking in self-control or devotion,
Nor to one who does not wish to hear,
Nor to one with negative emotion.

One who has supreme devotion
And teaches this philosophy
To those who love Me and follow,
Shall without question come to Me.

This is the highest service to Me,
So to Me, no one can be dearer.
And one who studies our sacred talk
Will through knowledge grow to Me nearer.

The one full of faith who hears this,
Having no doubt, and free from malice,
Will be liberated from all sin,
And reach the heaven of the righteous.

Arjuna, have you heard me clearly?
Has your delusion fallen away?
You are my chosen friend, and now
I've said all that there is to say.

ARJUNA:
Through your grace, O Krishna, I am firm.
I have regained my memory.
Delusion is gone, I am free from doubt.
To Your word, I will act accordingly.

GLOSSARY

Asvattha: The holy fig tree.

Atman: The Soul, the Self. Also the Spirit, that according to Advaita Vedanta is one with the individual soul.

Brahman: The Absolute. The Supreme Reality of Vedanta philosophy.

Dharma: Purpose. The law of inner being that nurtures the growth of a being and without which that being would cease to exist. Every being has its own dharma that determines its conduct, righteousness, and sense of right and wrong.

Gandiva: The name of Arjuna's bow.

Guna: The three human qualities, or tendencies: sattva, rajas, and tamas. Sattva represents balance and wisdom. Rajas represents activity and restlessness. Tamas represents inertia and dullness.

Japa: Practice where a name of God is said or thought in repetition.

Jnana: Knowledge.

Jnana Yoga: The path of knowledge.

Karma: Action. Duty.

Karma Yoga: The path of action, selfless service, work.

Maya: The cosmic illusion in which the One appears as many, and the Absolute appears as the relative.

Om: Also written as Aum. The most sacred word of the Vedas. The symbol of both the Personal God and the Absolute.
Prana: Breath. Life. The vital breath that sustains life in a physical body.

Rajas: The guna that represents activity and restlessness.

Sattva: The guna that represents balance and wisdom.

Tamas: The guna that represents inertia and dullness.

Vedanta: A system of philosophy discussed in the Upanishads, the Brahmasutras, and the Bhagavad Gita.

Vedas: The scriptures of the Hindu religion.

Vivaswat: Krishna's student, the sun god.

Yoga: Union. The union of the individual soul and the Supreme Soul. The practice and discipline through which this union takes place.

Yogi: One who practices yoga.

ACKNOWLEDGEMENTS

As Arjuna had Krishna to guide him, I have been fortunate to have had some wonderful teachers, generous with their wisdom, to help me along my path. Louise Taylor introduced me to the healing arts and to the yoga path. Deepak Chopra introduced me to Ayurveda and Vedanta. Vaidya Mishra deepened my spiritual understanding with the practice of Bhakti Yoga. And Swami Sarvadevananda continues to show me the value of spiritual commitment and community. I feel truly blessed - I love my family at the Vedanta Society.

In my career, I am grateful to have Bill Gladstone in my corner. And a big shout-out to Barbara Deal who is always so supportive. Thanks to Eric Woolf, who helps me so much with anything and everything technical. And thanks to Ophelia, Nancy, and Lindsay – they always have my back – and demonstrate what true friendship is all about.

Lots of love to my ever-growing family, and especially my dear husband, Greg, aka Dhamma Jyoti. I love having a spiritual partner by my side in this life's journey. Thank you for your love and support through all my adventures and endeavors!

And to Sri Ramakrishna, Sri Sarada Devi, and Swami Vivekananda – you are my family, too. Thank you for your words, your actions, your love, and your thoughtfulness. All of this helped to make the Song Divine come to be.

ABOUT THE AUTHOR

Lissa Coffey is a lifestyle and wellness expert and the founder of CoffeyTalk.com. Lissa is world renowned for her "Ancient Wisdom, Modern Style" philosophy. She has appeared on The Today Show, Good Morning America, HGTV, and many other national and local media outlets.

A best-selling author, Lissa has written several books, including the bestseller "What's Your Dosha, Baby? Discover the Vedic Way for Compatibility in Life and Love." Deepak Chopra says: "Coffey brings the timeless wisdom of Ayurveda to a contemporary audience and shows us how to discover more about ourselves and our relationships."

Lissa was honored with the Dharma Award from AAPNA for "Excellence in Promoting Awareness of Ayurveda." She was awarded a commendation for the Mayor of Los Angeles for her "Outstanding Contribution to the Yoga Community." She is a member of NAMA (National Ayurvedic Medical Association), and The Vedanta Society of Southern California. Lissa is a certified instructor with The Chopra Center.

Follow Lissa on Social Media

Facebook.com/LissaCoffeyTalk

Twitter.com/coffeytalk

Instagram.com/LissaCoffey

YouTube.com/coffeytalk

Learn about Ayurveda and Meditation

whatsyourdosha.com

Get Lissa's free email newsletters and more

coffeytalk.com

Other Titles by
LISSA COFFEY

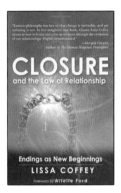

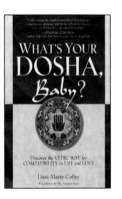

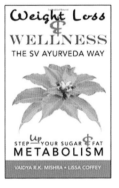

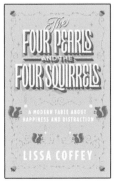

www.coffeytalk.com/books

LEARN ABOUT VEDANTA

vedanta.org

vedantahub.org

songdivine.com

79856440R00077

Made in the USA
Columbia, SC
31 October 2017